Happy Birthday

Anna von Marburg

A Sue Hines Book
Allen & Unwin

Acknowledgements

Thank You God for the talent.
Thanks to my beautiful children Jack, Georgina and Mary for completing my 'circle of life'.
Thank you to Ommie, my mother-in-law and great friend.
Thank you to my mother, father, family and friends for shamelessly supporting me and bragging about my work.
Thank you Chiara and the Focolare who have taught me that time is love.
Thank you Simon, my wonderful photographer and friend.
Thank you Carolyn Simm, for your support and brilliant style.
Thank you Sue Hines and Allen & Unwin for publishing this fabulous little book!

First published in 2000
A Sue Hines Book
Allen & Unwin Pty Ltd
9 Atchison Street
St Leonards NSW 1590 Australia
Phone: (61 2) 8425 0100
Fax: (61 2) 9906 2218
E-mail: frontdesk@allen-unwin.com.au
Web: http://www.allen-unwin.com.au

National Library of Australia
Cataloguing-in-Publication entry:

Von Marburg, Anna.
Happy birthday.

ISBN 1 86508 144 2.

1. Cake decorating. 2. Cake. I. Title.

641. 8653

Designed by Carolyn Simm, Simm Design
Photography by Simon Griffiths
Typeset by Neil Conning & Associates
Printed in Hong Kong through Phoenix Offset

For Rollie, my love, who still calls me 'Gorgeous', which ain't bad for a girl's self-esteem.

Contents

Introduction

Growing up as one of ten children gave me a lot of practice at birthday cakes. Mom wasn't crazy about baking cakes so she let me do just about anything I wanted in the kitchen, providing I cleaned up and didn't lose any body parts. I began as a Betty Crocker cake-mix kid, then learned to make cakes from scratch. I liked baking, but I *loooved* decorating. It was never anything elaborate, just flat cakes with writing, piped flowers, and various shapes on them. Eventually, when I was seventeen, I was so bold as to make my sister Patty's wedding cake. It tasted delicious, had about a bottle of apricot brandy in it, and looked beautiful decorated with full-blown peony roses from my grandfather's garden. It fell onto the pavement. I was mortified. Mom and Patty went down the driveway and salvaged what they could. I think I was hiding in a corner crying when they came in. They just kept saying how wonderful it tasted as they lovingly reassembled it! That's my mom and Patty for you. Because of their response to my failure, I am now a professional cake decorator and not in an asylum.

Now when it's birthday time around our house, I'm just like any other mother who doesn't have a huge amount of spare time to make cakes for family and friends. I've designed the cakes in this book for those times when style is important but convenience is paramount. Almost all the ingredients for these designs are easily obtained at the supermarket. Almost all the cakes can be made three days in advance (if you use my recipes) and stored at room temperature so that you aren't moving the deli meats and condiments into the garage to make room in the refrigerator for the cake! Last but not least, these designs are quick . . . once the cake is baked, it shouldn't take more than an hour or two to decorate.

Some people know that I decorate cakes for a living so they often come up to me at a park or playground looking like a repentant sinner at confession to tell me how they made their child's birthday cake and what a fiasco it was. These fiascos always have one or two things in common . . . they failed to plan and tried to make the cake an hour before the party when the children were blowing party horns in their ears (sorry, I can't help you with that one) or they couldn't figure out how to frost a cake without getting crumbs in the frosting (that one I can help you with, see page 92, Crumbs). So, may I suggest that you please read the Basics before making any of the cakes. There is valuable information in there.

Please enjoy yourself. Don't get flustered . . . remember the cake love story from above and what really matters!

back to nature

Unpotted

This is a simple version of a design from *Cakes in Bloom* using a real sunflower instead of a hand-sculpted sugar flower. You can, of course, use any flower, but one big happy sunflower just seems right to me.

F or fun, serve the cake on a clean garden tile instead of the traditional cake plate.

Ingredients

- 4 round chocolate fudge cakes,
each 15 cm (6 in) across and 3 cm (1¼ in) high
- 2 quantities chocolate butter (page 93)
- ½ quantity crumbcoat frosting (page 92)
- green food colouring
- piping bag, round tip
- 1 pesticide-free sunflower (wrap the part of the stalk that will be inserted into the cake with plastic wrap or aluminium foil)

Instructions

Stack the cakes on top of each other, filling between the layers with half the chocolate butter.

Carve the sides down with a thin, sharp knife to resemble a 'pot' shape as shown. In a food processor, pulse the leftover pieces of cake into crumbs and set aside. Spread the remaining chocolate butter over the cake.

Colour the frosting green (see page 96). Fill a piping bag fitted with a round tip with the frosting. Pipe 'root' systems around the cake starting at the top edge and fading to the bottom. Allow the cake to rest for about 15 minutes until the green frosting hardens slightly and forms a thin crust.

Scoop handfuls of chocolate crumbs around the sides and on top of the cake, pressing gently into the sides. The crumbs shouldn't stick to the green roots because of the crust that has formed.

Use the handle of a wooden spoon or similar object to gently make a hole in the top of the cake for the sunflower stem. Just before serving, position the sunflower on the cake. Remove the flower before serving.

These are the sweetest little treats to send along to kindergarten on your child's birthday. The children marvel at the little clumps of chocolate earth with mint 'seedlings' popping out the top. It encourages a good sense of humour at an early age.

Ingredients

- 12 cupcakes (chocolate with a dash of mint extract is wonderful)★
- 2 quantities chocolate butter (page 93) at liquid pouring consistency
- hard chocolate biscuits (cookies) to grind up as 'dirt' or a few extra chocolate cupcakes
- 12 mint sprigs
- mini greenhouse

★ Bake cupcakes in a cupcake tin with or without papers. Make sure to grease the tins well if you are not using papers. If you bake the cupcakes with papers, remove the papers before rolling in the chocolate butter and crumbs.

Instructions

Pulse the chocolate biscuits (cookies) or extra cupcakes into crumbs in a food processor.

Dip the cupcakes into the chocolate butter to coat them (do not allow it to thicken to spreading consistency—if it does, just reheat it). Allow the cupcakes to rest on a wire rack for a few minutes until the chocolate stops dripping, then roll them in the chocolate crumbs.

Just before serving, use a toothpick to poke a little hole in the top of the cupcake and insert the mint sprig.

Another Idea

Instead of the mint sprigs, use small, edible, unsprayed, pesticide-free fresh flowers, such as apple, orange or lemon blossom, violets, lilacs, pansies, petunias, nasturtiums or roses.

Bzzzzz

As a child, I could never eat one of those yellow–and–black striped licorice allsorts without thinking of *bumblebees*.

A recipe that requires a Dolly Varden cake tin (pan). This type of tin is usually used to make the bottom half (the skirt section) of a doll cake. A doll's head is then plugged into this cake section to make Dolly Varden. The cake part is a wonderful chubby little shape, but if you don't have one of these cake tins, you can use 3 round cakes, each 18 cm (7 in) across, and carve them into this shape.

Ingredients

• 1 Dolly Varden cake base or 3 round cakes,
each 18 cm (7 in) across and 3.5 cm (1½ in) high
• 1 quantity topcoat frosting (page 92) (if you are using three 18 cm (7 in)
cakes you'll need a total of 1½ quantities topcoat frosting)
• 1 tsp instant coffee, dissolved
in 1 tsp boiling water, cooled to room temperature
• piping bag, round or other tip
• yellow–and–black striped licorice allsorts (candy)
• rice paper or gelatine sheets (available in baking section of supermarket)
• craft wire
• small brush
• 1 tbsp honey

Instructions

To make the bumblebees, carve the licorice pieces into a fat cylindrical shape with a thin, sharp knife. Slice a little 'v' indent into the top of the cylinder to place the wings. Cut the wings out of the rice paper or gelatine sheets with a pair of scissors. Very lightly brush water or frosting into the 'v' indent on the top of the bumblebee and attach the wings. Stick tiny pieces of black licorice to the front of the bee with a dab of frosting for the bee's eyes. Coil some craft wire by wrapping it around a pencil or dowel rod then insert the wire into the bottom of the bumblebee.

Colour the frosting with the food colouring or coffee mixture.

If you use the three 18 cm (7 in) round cakes, stack them on top of each other and fill between the layers with frosting. Carve the cake into the shape of the beehive using a thin, sharp knife.

Spread a thin layer of frosting around the cake. Cut a little beehive 'entrance' at the base of the cake.

Fill a piping bag fitted with a round tip (or any tip) with the remaining frosting. (If you have a cake turntable or lazy Susan, now's the time to bring it out.) Starting at the base of the cake, pipe coils of frosting around the cake until it is completely covered. If you're using the turntable or lazy Susan, keep your piping bag *steady* and *move* the lazy Susan with the other hand.

Place a spoonful of honey at the entrance of the beehive.

Position your bumblebees on the cake. Remove the bumblebee wires before serving.

Topiary Tops

These topiary cakes are perfect for a party in the garden. For some fun, place one of these simply decorated cakes in *the garden* amongst some real topiary pots before the party begins.

During the party, when you're ready to bring out the birthday cake and ice-cream, simply pull one of these little pots from the garden and plant some candles on top!

You can achieve all sorts of different textures by using various tips on your piping bag (star, leaf, round) or create other textures by simply frosting the cake with a spatula and applying green coconut or sugar.

To make one topiary cake

Ingredients

- 2 round cakes, each 18 cm (7 in) across and 3.5 cm (1½ in) high
- 1½ quantities topcoat frosting (page 92)
- green food colouring (preferably paste or powdered)
- piping bag, any tip
- assorted sweets or candy for decorations
- 1 round piece of cardboard 18 cm (7 in) across
- terracotta pot (the diameter of the top of the pot should be slightly smaller than the diameter of your cake, for example 15 cm/6 in)

Instructions

Stack the cakes on top of each other, filling between the layers with some of the frosting. Place the cake on the cardboard.

Colour the remaining frosting green (see page 96) and spread a thin layer on the cake.

Fill a piping bag fitted with the tip of your choice (leaf, star, round, etc.) with the remaining green frosting and pipe individual leaves, stars, dots or other shapes all over the cake. It you are piping dots, they will have a point on them. If you want to get rid of the point, wrap a slightly damp (not wet) cloth around the end of your index finger and flatten each point.

Place the cake on the pot. The green of the frosting can sometimes bleed into the decorations so if you are not serving the cake within the next hour or so, place the piping bag containing the leftover frosting in an airtight container. An hour or so before presenting the cake, pipe small dots onto the cake where you want to place the decorations and press the decorations onto the dot of frosting.

More Ideas

- Write your Happy Birthday message on the pot with a marker first.
- Make sugar daisies for these cakes. See the Cupcake Tree, page 27, for instructions on how to make them.
- Miniature topiary cakes made with cupcakes are delightful.
- Pots. There are zillions of varieties of terracotta, plastic and cement pots available. I painted the terracotta pots for the cakes shown with acrylic craft paints. Go wild making wonderful designs on your pots (numbers and ABCs) . . . or go wild decorating the cake and keep your pot simple. Miniature pots are available from craft shops and garden shops.
- Cake decorations can include fresh edible flowers; jelly beans; balls of bubble gum; sugared violets, lilacs and roses; hand-sculpted sugar flowers or rose petals; marzipan fruits . . . just to get you started.
- Fill the pots with sweets or candy—snakes, worms, or any other sugar versions of little creatures you might find under a bush (see picture on facing page).

Sunflower

My son *Jack* and I planted some sunflowers at our front porch step this year and every time we walk by them we say hello. They seem so human that we've discussed giving them little chocolate eyes and a mouth so they can speak to us.

I baked an 18 cm (7 in) round cake for this design but you can of course make it as big as you like. I used the chocolate fudge cake because, although it's small, it's rich and a little goes a long way. You can roll out the yellow sugar dough, cut and apply the sunflower petals as you are decorating the cake, but if I have time the day before, I like to make at least half of the petals in advance so that they have time to dry and add a more 3D appearance to the petals.

Ingredients

- 1 round cake 18 cm (7 in) across and approximately 3.5 cm (1½ in) high
- 1 quantity chocolate butter (page 93)
- piping bag, round tip
- 2 tbsp yellow sugar (page 96)

Sunflower Petals

- 1 quantity or more sugar dough (page 94)
  or quick sugar dough (page 95)
- yellow food colouring (preferably paste or powder)
- corn husk (preferably dried) or other leaf for veining sunflower petals
- 300 g (10 oz) box cornflour (cornstarch)

Instructions

Make the sugar petals one day in advance if possible (see facing page). Otherwise, proceed as follows.

Round the top edge of the cake with a thin, sharp knife. Spread a thin layer of the chocolate butter on the cake and place it on your serving plate.

If you have made some or all of the petals in advance, place them around the perimeter of the cake now. If you haven't made the petals in advance, follow the instructions on page 23 for making the petals, skipping the part about placing them on the baking tray of cornflour and drying. Place a row of the petals around the perimeter of the base of the cake. Twist them gently onto themselves and the serving plate to give them movement. Once you have a complete circle of petals around the base of the cake, add another row of petals on top of this row, gently giving them movement once again. (The sugar dough will be the consistency of play dough, so it will hold a few twists without flopping onto itself.) I like to intersperse dried petals with some soft ones to make them fit together nicely.

Fill a piping bag fitted with a round tip with some of the remaining chocolate butter and pipe dots all over the cake, beginning in the centre and working your way out. Don't fill the bag too full because the heat from your hand can make the chocolate butter too soft to pipe. If this happens, put the piping bag aside to cool down.

For an added touch, carefully spoon some yellow sugar crystals just where the chocolate dots meet the sugar petals.

Sunflower Petals

Ideally, make these petals a day or more in advance.

Colour the sugar dough yellow (page 96). Line a baking tray with cornflour to hold the drying petals. Roll out the sugar dough (the thinner, the more life-like), using cornflour to keep it from sticking to yours hands, rolling pin and work surface. Cut petal-shaped pieces in various sizes using a thin, sharp knife. For this cake size the petals vary in length from approximately 3.5 to 8 cm (1½ to 3 in). While the petals are still soft, press them against the corn husk or leaf to give them life-like veins. Dip your fingers in plenty of cornflour and smooth the edges of the petals between your fingers to give them 'movement'. Place them on the baking tray to dry for a day (or straight onto the cake if you do not have time). Once dry, dust the cornflour off the petals before placing them around the cake.

More Ideas

- Pipe a happy face in the centre of the cake.
- If you have 'pipophobia' (fear of piping) arrange chocolate chips on the cake instead of piping the chocolate dots.
- If you're feeling artistic (and you will be), mix up different shades of yellow and orange and dilute with vodka. Brush lightly onto the petals beginning in the centre and fading out as you move to the outer edges.
- For glossy petals, lightly brush them, or sections of them, with vegetable oil or sugar syrup.

Cupcake Tree

A cupcake tree is like a *croquembouche* but without the fuss. Simply bake little cupcakes in papers, frost them, skewer them onto a styrofoam cone shape and decorate. I have taken some time to make little sugar daisies for this design, but you can use real edible flowers.

If you want to use sugar daisies, you'll need to make them at least the day before so they have time to dry. If it's humid, they may take two or three days to dry. They are very fragile when they are dry, so handle them carefully. You can buy styrofoam cones at craft shops or florist-supply shops. Any size can work, but I've given the measurements for the one I used with this design.

Ingredients

- 25 or more miniature cupcakes, each approximately 3.5 cm (1½ in) across and 2.5 cm (1 in) high
- 25 toothpicks or bamboo skewers
- 1 quantity topcoat frosting (page 92)
- orange food colouring
- styrofoam cone 25 cm (10 in) high and 10 cm (4 in) wide at the base

Sugar Daisies

- 1 quantity sugar dough (page 94) or quick sugar dough (page 95)
- yellow food colouring
- 300 g (10 oz) box cornflour (cornstarch)
- 10 toothpicks
- at least 2 tbsp yellow sugar (page 96)
- daisy or blossom shape cutter

Instructions

Make the sugar daisies one day in advance (see below).

Colour the frosting a very pale orange (peach), then spread on each of the cupcakes.

Insert a toothpick or bamboo skewer through each of the cupcakes to attach it to the styrofoam cone. Begin by placing the cupcakes around the base of the cone and work your way up.

Place the daisies on the cupcakes, ideally while frosting is still soft. They should adhere directly to the cupcake. If the frosting has set, put a dab of soft frosting on the back of the daisy. Use the daisies on toothpicks to fill in any gaps. Remove the toothpicks before serving.

Sugar Daisies

Line a baking tray with the cornflour to hold the drying petals. Set aside a small piece of sugar dough and colour it yellow for the daisy centres. Roll out the remaining sugar dough (the thinner, the more life-like) using cornflour to keep it from sticking to your hands, rolling pin, the work surface and cutters. Cut approximately 30 daisies from the dough. Roll little balls of yellow sugar dough and attach to the daisy centres with a small amount of water. Place the daisies on the baking tray to dry. Wrap any leftover sugar dough in plastic wrap and store in an airtight container. Allow the daisies to dry for at least 24 hours. They can sit on the baking tray at room temperature for at least a month, although high humidity may make them flop. They can also be stored in a box, but not in an airtight container: they need to 'breathe'.

Once dry, lightly dust them off with a soft brush. Paint the yellow daisy centres with water and sprinkle with yellow sugar.

A few dry daisies on toothpicks are useful for filling any gaps in the styrofoam. To do this, attach a little ball of soft sugar dough to the back of the daisy with some water, then dip a toothpick in water and insert it into this little ball at the back of the daisy.

Gathered Wild Roses

I make versions of this cake with one, two, three or more tiers for celebrations, usually with hand-sculpted sugar flowers, but you can use *fresh* full-blown roses from the garden for this quick version.

A small version of my most popular creation, the Gathered Wild Roses Cake, which features a tall cylindrical-shaped cake with stems and leaves growing up the side, crowned with a profusion of flowers. You will need a dense cake to hold the weight of the flowers.

Ingredients

• 4 round chocolate fudge cakes (page 90),
each 15 cm (6 in) across and 3 cm (1¼ in) high
• 1 quantity chocolate butter (page 93)
• 1½ quantities topcoat frosting (page 92) or ½ quantity crumbcoat
frosting (page 92) and 1 quantity topcoat frosting
• green food colouring
• piping bag, round, leaf, or other suitable tip
• half a ball of florist foam★ (usually green, sometimes called Oasis)
• fresh pesticide-free roses

★ Buy a whole ball and cut it in half, or you can round off a block of florist
foam into a hemisphere with a thin, sharp knife if you can't find a ball.

Instructions

Stack the cakes on top of each other, filling between the layers with the chocolate butter.

Make the topcoat frosting and set aside ¾ cup for piping the stems.

Spread the topcoat frosting on the cake or, for a crumb-free frosting, first spread a thin layer of crumbcoat frosting on the cake and allow it to harden slightly for approximately an hour to 'set' the crumbs. Then spread the topcoat frosting on the cake (see page 92, Crumbs).

Colour the reserved ¾ cup topcoat frosting green and fill a piping bag fitted with a round tip with the frosting. Pipe stems down the side of cake, moving the piping bag every few centimetres to give the stem a little 'knob' like a real rose stem. Change tips and pipe small leaves on the stems (use a leaf tip or pipe leaf outlines with a round tip and fill them in).

Wrap the half ball of florist foam in plastic wrap so it doesn't touch the frosting and place it on the top of the cake, flat side down. Insert the flowers into the foam, starting at the base and filling in the top as you proceed. Remove flowers and foam before serving.

More Ideas

• To make a double-decker version of this cake, use the instructions for the
Double-decker Ice-cream Feast cake on page 41.

• Tie a ribbon around the middle of the cake, as in the Ice-cream
Feast cake (page 38).

• For take-home gifts, offer 'big girls' miniature bouquets of roses. For little
girls, give them the same bouquets but wire little sweets or candies into the
bouquet. Use cellophane-wrapped sweets and craft wire or florist wire.
Twist the wire around the cellophane ends.

I f you take the children camping for their birthday, or even just light up a camp fire in your backyard at night and *pretend* you're camping, this cake is fast, simple, and of course goes with the theme!

Ingredients

• 3 round cakes (butter cakes or denser),
each 18 cm (7 in) across and 3.5 cm (1½ in) high
• 1½ quantities chocolate butter (page 93) or topcoat frosting (page 92)
• assorted marshmallows (vanilla and toasted coconut shown)
• twigs from trees (non-poisonous!) or bamboo skewers
• bandanna

Instructions

Stack the cakes on top of each other, filling between the layers with some of the chocolate butter or frosting. Spread the remaining chocolate butter or frosting all over the cake.

Skewer the marshmallows on the twigs or bamboo skewers and place them around the sides of the cake. They should adhere slightly to the frosting.

Fill in the top of the cake with marshmallows.

Tie a bandanna around the middle of the cake. Remove sticks or skewers before serving.

birthdays are made
of this

Diaper

An ideal baby's first birthday cake
or a 'graduation' cake from wearing
diapers.

For take-home treats for the guests, wrap up pieces of leftover cake or chocolates in plastic wrap, then wrap 'diaper style' in pieces of flannel cloth and secure with a real diaper pin.

Ingredients

- 1 cake, 30 cm long, 20 cm wide and 3.5 cm high (12 × 8 × 1½ in)
- ¾ quantity chocolate butter (page 93) or topcoat frosting (page 92)
- 1½ quantities rolled fondant (page 93)
(three 500 g/1 lb boxes, if purchasing)
- sifted pure icing sugar (confectioner's sugar) for dusting work surface
- blue, red and green food colouring

Instructions

Cut the cake in half so that you have two cakes 20 cm long and 15 cm wide (8 × 6 in). Cut the cake into a 15 cm (6 in) square. (Eat the off-cut for a snack.)

Stack the cakes on top of each other, filling between the layers with some of the chocolate butter or frosting. Spread the remaining chocolate butter or frosting on the cake.

Dust your work surface generously with the sifted sugar. Knead the rolled fondant until it is nice and smooth. Form it into a ball and begin to flatten it with your hands into a square. Use the rolling pin to roll it into a large square. After every few rolls, shift the rolled fondant to keep it from sticking to the surface, then use your hands to shape it into a square. Once the square is approximately 38 cm (15 in) wide, use a thin, sharp knife to cut it into a nice clean 38 cm (15 in) square. Save a leftover piece of rolled fondant to make your diaper pin.

Position the rolled fondant on the work surface so that it looks like a diamond shape. Position the cake on the rolled fondant so that it looks like a square on a diamond.

Fold the top edge of the rolled fondant over the cake, then the left side, the right side, and finally fold the bottom side up over all of them.

Colour a piece of the leftover rolled fondant blue to make the plastic head of the diaper pin. Colour another piece of the leftover rolled fondant with a mixture of blue, red, and green to achieve a greyish colour for the metal part of the diaper pin.

Don't dust off the sifted sugar—it resembles baby powder!

Ice-cream Feast

Perplexed expressions give way to gleeful shouts of *'I can do that'* whenever I demonstrate making this cake. It may look tricky to you, until you realise that the ice-cream cones are simply cut in half and then attached directly to the frosting.

Y ou will need a dense cake such as the chocolate fudge cake for this creation to hold the weight of the ice-cream. Make sure you have a proper ice-cream scoop with a release lever on the side for nice round scoops.

Ingredients

- 4 round chocolate fudge cakes (page 90), each 15 cm (6 in) across and 3 cm (1¼ in) high
- 1 quantity chocolate butter (page 93)
- 1½ quantities topcoat frosting (page 92)
or ½ quantity crumbcoat frosting (page 92) and 1 quantity topcoat frosting
- 5 full traditional ice-cream cones, approximately 12.5 cm (5 in) long (not waffle, they crumble)
- ribbon
- 2 litres (2.2 quarts) assorted ice-creams

Instructions

To cut the ice-cream cones in half, position the cone on a work surface with the pointed end up. Starting at the pointed end, use a thin serrated knife (a steak knife is perfect) to slice it in half using a gentle sawing action.

Stack the cakes on top of each other, filling between the layers with the chocolate butter.

Spread the topcoat frosting on the cake or, for a crumb-free frosting first spread a thin layer of crumbcoat frosting on the cake and allow it to harden slightly for approximately an hour to 'set' the crumbs. Then spread the topcoat frosting on the cake (see page 92, Crumbs).

While the topcoat frosting is still soft, attach the halved ice-cream cones to the cake, keeping the flat end of the cone flush with the top of the cake. If the cones are too long for the cake, slice some off the top of the cone with the serrated knife.

Tie a ribbon around the cake, pulling it snugly around the cones, then tie a bow. You may want to insert a toothpick just under the bow to help hold the ribbon in place. (Remember to remove the toothpick before serving.)

Make approximately twenty scoops of ice-cream and place them on a baking tray in the freezer until you are ready to use them. Just before serving, pop them on top of the cake.

In addition to the four 15 cm (6 in) cakes, which will become the top tier of your double-decker cake, you will need:

Ingredients

• 4 round chocolate fudge cakes, each 23 cm (9 in) across
(to form the bottom tier of your double-decker cake)
• extra chocolate butter
• extra 9 full ice-cream cones, cut in half
• 3 pencil-thin dowel rods the same height as the 23 cm (9 in) cake stack
• ribbons
• ice-cream

Stack the larger cakes on top of each other and fill between the layers with chocolate butter. Insert the dowel rods vertically into the stack an equal distance apart, 5 cm (2 in) in from the edge of the stack. Place the stack of four smaller cakes on a heavy round cardboard base 15 cm (6 in) across and place the entire small stack (cardboard included) on top of the large stack of cakes. Spread frosting over the entire cake, attach the ice-cream cones, tie the ribbons and place the scoops of ice-cream on the cake as shown.

More Ideas

I have done many versions of this cake, but here are a few favourites.
• Dress up this cake for a glamorous dinner party by covering the cake in chocolate butter, gilding the cones in 24 carat gold or silver leaf, and scooping different shades of frozen chocolate mousse (white, milk and dark) on top.
• Dip the cones in shades of melted chocolate then dip again in sugar sprinkles or beads, and little edible sugar silver and gold balls. Or roll the scoops of ice-cream in the sugar sprinkles and beads.
• Place square ice-cream cones upright on a baking tray and half fill the cones with cake batter. Bake in a 180°C (350°F) oven for approximately 15 minutes. Allow to cool completely, then top with a scoop of ice-cream for a cake and ice-cream all in one.
• For a take-home treat, fill an ice-cream cone with little sweets and place a big chocolate-covered marshmallow biscuit (cookie) at the top of the cone to resemble a scoop of ice-cream. Wrap it in clear cellophane and tie with a ribbon.

Lollipop, Lollipop

When I was three years old my parents took all *ten* of us children to an amusement park, then left the park without me. It was an honest mistake, they said. I don't remember feeling traumatised at all. All I do remember is eating one of these great big lollipops as I waited for them.

If the small lollipop sticks are too long, cut them so that the lollipop and stick are the same height as the assembled cake. Cut the stick off the large lollipop. You may need a small saw if they are wooden sticks.

Ingredients

- 4 round cakes (butter cakes or denser), each 15 cm (6 in) across and 3 cm ($1\frac{1}{4}$ in) high
- 2 quantities topcoat frosting (page 92) or $\frac{1}{2}$ quantity crumbcoat frosting and $1\frac{1}{2}$ quantities topcoat frosting (page 92)
- approximately 10 lollipops 9 cm ($3\frac{1}{2}$ in) wide
- 1 lollipop 14 cm ($5\frac{1}{2}$ in) wide
- ribbon

Instructions

Stack the cakes on top of each other, filling between the layers with some of the topccat frosting.

Spread the topcoat frosting on the cake or, for a crumb-free frosting, first spread a thin layer of crumbcoat frosting on the cake and allow it to harden slightly for approximately an hour to 'set' the crumbs. Then spread the topcoat frosting on the cake (see page 92, Crumbs).

Place the large lollipop on the top of the cake. Press the small lollipops into the sides of the cake as shown.

Tie a ribbon around the middle of the cake.

Hannah

You don't need to be a professional artist or sculptor to make this cake because all the hard work has already been done for you. This cherub cake was created by lining a plastic *cherub mould* with rolled fondant, then filling it with crumbs from a moist *baked* cake.

I have designed a range of plastic moulds like Hannah but there are plastic craft moulds, cake tins, jelly and mousse moulds, in a range of shapes and sizes which can be used in the same way.

You will need a very rich, moist, *baked* cake base for this design. The chocolate fudge cake recipe is ideal, as are most mud cake, chocolate torte, and similar recipes. If you want to use a recipe other than the chocolate fudge cake, test it first by pulsing a piece of the baked cake in a food processor until it forms a ball. If it doesn't form a ball, it will need to be moistened with sugar syrup (page 95) or some melted butter or both. However, it is best to use a cake that is already moist enough and forms a ball without any more added moisteners.

Ingredients

- 1 round chocolate fudge cake (page 90), 25 cm (10 in) across and 3 cm (1¼ in) high
- 1 quantity rolled fondant (two 500 g/1 lb boxes, if purchasing)★
- sifted pure icing sugar (confectioner's sugar) for dusting work surface

★ You will have 300–400 g (10–10½ oz) left over, but this gives you room for adjustment. Do not use the microwave method described in Basics to soften the rolled fondant because you may make it too soft and sticky and cause it to stick to the mould.

Instructions

Make sure you allow the cake to cool completely before using.

Break the *baked* cake into six or more pieces and pulse each piece in a food processor until it breaks into small pieces and forms a ball. If you don't have a food processor, you can cut up the pieces very finely with a knife and then knead them into a ball. If the chocolate fudge cake is not forming a ball and seems dry for some reason, add some melted butter until it forms a ball. Set aside.

Dust your rolling pin and work surface generously with the sifted sugar. Knead the rolled fondant until it is nice and smooth. Form it into a ball and begin to flatten it with your hands into a circle (or to the shape of your mould). Use the rolling pin to finish the rolling. Ideally, the rolled fondant should be approximately 1 cm (½ in) thick, but if this is your first time working with it you may want to make it thicker so it's easier to handle.

Measure your mould and make sure your piece of rolled fondant is slightly larger than the mould.

Dust the mould generously with the sifted sugar then fold the rolled fondant over the rolling pin and lift it onto the mould. Ease the rolled fondant into the mould, gently pressing it into the details of the cherub.

Press the baked chocolate fudge cake mixture into the mould until it is level with the top of the mould (slightly less is better than too much mixture). Trim the excess rolled fondant with a thin, sharp knife then use your fingers to smooth any ragged bits of rolled fondant in towards the cake mixture. Invert onto your cake plate at once. If it sticks, hold the inverted mould firmly on the plate and tap it on the counter to help loosen it.

If you have any cracks, dents or wrinkles, mix up a paste of the sifted sugar and water and rub this mixture into any imperfections. These cakes are rarely ever beyond repair . . . as I tell my students, 'a mistake is an opportunity to be creative'.

To finish it off, lightly brush the cake with water, then sprinkle white sugar over it for texture. This also helps hide any wrinkles or folds for 'first timers'.

More Ideas

- Lightly paint the cherub with food colouring diluted with vodka.
- Gild the cake in 22-carat gold or silver leaf (available at art-supply shops, Asian grocers, pastry-supply shops). To do this, brush the cake lightly with sugar syrup or water and apply the sheets of gold or silver leaf.
- Add a few drops of food colouring to the rolled fondant and knead it a few times, allowing streaks to remain. When you roll it out, it will have a marbled appearance.

Silver Service

Every *child's dream* and every parent's nightmare—a full-course sit-down meal of sweets and candy!

Have a dining-room table beautifully set in a room away from the birthday party where the children won't see it. Give them only savoury foods throughout the party: hot dogs, hamburgers, you know the routine. Have them starved for sugar, then usher them into the 'dining room' and listen to them groan as they have to sit down for a 'big person's' meal. Then voila! Out come the goodies.

At breakfast on the morning of their birthday, offer your child a chocolate egg in a beautiful egg cup instead of the usual 'toast and poached egg' . . . they'll wonder what's going on.

Menu

Traditional Pasta
with Red Sauce and Meatballs
(six-metre bubble gum roll sliced up with a piece of red dehydrated
fruit snack and chocolate malt balls)

Fresh Green Salad with Baby Tomatoes
(spearmint leaves and raspberry chews)

Whole Roasted Baby Potatoes
(balls of marzipan rolled in cocoa)

Fresh Milk
(milk bottle chews)

Coffee
(half-melted chocolate, half milk)

Fruit
(marzipan fruit)

For a Successful Dinner Party

To keep your sanity, offer this meal in the last half hour of the party, then send the children home to their own parents.

Have mercy on the children: offer 'doggie bags' so they can take home what they can't eat at the 'meal'.

After this meal, there's no need for a birthday cake, but if you would still like the 'happy birthday' ceremony, a silver candelabra is perfect for holding candles for the birthday boy or girl to blow out. Alternatively, offer them a silver tray of candles in candle holders or attach small birthday candles with dots of melted wax to a silver tray.

I nstead of candles on top of a birthday cake, why not make the candles a feature around the cake?

Ingredients

- 4 round cakes (butter cakes or denser), each 15 cm (6 in) across and 3 cm (1¼ in) high
- 1½ quantities topcoat frosting (page 92)
- yellow sugar (page 96)
- approximately 18 candles, each 15 cm (6 in) long or longer
- coloured raffia

Instructions

Stack the cakes on top of each other, filling between the layers with the frosting.

Spread the frosting on the cake. Sprinkle the yellow sugar on top of the cake. Position the candles around the cake. They should adhere to the frosting, but it might be easier to have someone help you hold them in place. Tie the coloured raffia around the middle of the cake. Remove the candles before serving.

down by the sea

Sandcastle

You can make this as a baked cake, as I've done here, or as an *ice-cream* cake by packing softened ice-cream into your child's sand bucket and refreezing it.

The cake is covered in white and light-brown sugar and the starfish are made out of sugar dough, then painted with food colouring in wonderful shades of the sea. The starfish need to be made at least a day in advance so they have time to dry out enough to be painted.

Ingredients

- 4 round chocolate fudge cakes (page 90), each 18 cm (7 in) across and 3 cm (1¼ in) high
- 1 quantity chocolate butter (page 93)
- 1 quantity topcoat frosting (page 92)
- approximately 500 g (1 lb) mixture of light-brown sugar and white sugar
- sweets or candy for decorations of doors, windows etc.

Sugar Starfish

- 1 or more quantities sugar dough (page 94) or quick sugar dough (page 95)
- 300 g (10 oz) box cornflour (cornstarch)
- food colouring
- vodka or water
- dowel rods (pencil thickness or less) or bamboo skewers
- soft brush and paint brush
- various sized star cutters

Instructions

Make the sugar starfish one day in advance (see page 61).

Stack the cakes on top of each other, filling between the layers with chocolate butter.

Carve the sides of the cake with a thin, sharp knife to resemble an upside-down sand bucket. The top should measure approximately 13 cm (5 in) in diameter and the bottom will remain 18 cm (7 in) in diameter.

Spread the frosting on the cake. Press handfuls of the sugar 'sand' mixture into the sides and top of the cake.

Press any sweets or candy decorations into the cake to make windows, doors and other decorations. Decorate with the starfish. Remove starfish and dowels before serving.

Sugar Starfish

Line a baking tray with the cornflour to hold the drying starfish.

Roll out the sugar dough to a thickness of approximately 1 cm (½ in), using cornflour to keep the dough from sticking to your hands, rolling pin, work surface and cutters. Cut star shapes. Squeeze and pull at each of the points to elongate them into starfish legs.

Dip a dowel rod into some water, then insert it into the starfish. (You may want to sharpen the dowel rods first with a pencil sharpener.)

Lay the starfish on the baking tray to dry. Lay them so they aren't perfectly flat and have lots of movement.

The next day, lightly dust off the starfish with a soft brush. Mix up some wonderful sea colours using food colouring diluted with vodka. The vodka helps to dry the food colouring more quickly than water but, as a last resort, you can use water. Use a paint brush to lightly brush the colour onto the starfish.

More Ideas

• If you are in a rush and don't have time to make the starfish out of sugar, there are lots of sweets or candy in seashell and starfish shapes, which you can place on skewers instead.

• For take-home treats, fill sea shells with little surprises and wrap them in cellophane, then tie with dried seaweed or raffia.

• Bring out sand buckets filled with ice-cream or fruit to accompany the cake.

• To make this design as an ice-cream cake, fill a sand bucket with softened ice-cream, then freeze. Unmould the bucket and allow the ice-cream to soften slightly (or run a hot spatula around the cake) and apply handfuls of the brown sugar mixture and the sweets or candy for decorations. Refreeze until ready to serve.

Fish Tank

Quite *unconventional*, I know, but children love it. How do you do it? Well, first you attach sugar decorations to the sides of the tank. Then you lower in the cake (which is just slightly smaller than the tank), then fill in the gap between the tank and the cake with blue sugar.

Y ou can adjust the dimensions of this cake to fit the size and shape of the fish tank you use. There should be a 1 cm (½ in) clearance between the tank and the cake. Try other themes such as mermaids, killer piranhas, sharks and pirates.

Ingredients

- fish tank 29 cm long, 18 cm wide and 16 cm high (12 × 7 × 6 in)
- three cakes 33 cm long, 23 cm wide and 3.5 cm high (13 × 9 × 1½ in)
- 2 quantities chocolate butter (page 93) or topcoat frosting (page 92)
- 1 or more quantities of rolled fondant (page 93), sugar dough (page 94), or quick sugar dough (page 95)
- sifted pure icing sugar (confectioner's sugar) for dusting work surface
- food colouring (preferably paste or powdered)
- approximately 2 kg (5 lb) blue sugar (page 95)
- heavy cardboard cut to the size of the cake base
- kitchen string

Instructions

Colour the rolled fondant, sugar dough, or quick sugar dough the desired colours. Roll it out using the sifted sugar to prevent it from sticking to your rolling pin, work surface, knife or cutters. Use a thin, sharp knife to cut out decorations of fish, seaweed, or any other underwater life. Brush one side of the decoration lightly with water and attach it to the tank.

Stack the cakes on top of each other, filling between the layers with chocolate butter or frosting. Measure your fish tank and cut down the sides of the cake to fit the tank, allowing approximately 1 cm (½ in) clearance between the cake and the tank on all sides. Place the stack of cakes on a piece of heavy cardboard the same size as the cake base.

Place two lengths of kitchen string underneath the cardboard and up each side of the cake, then gently lower the cake, cardboard and all, into the tank. (Think of a crane at the docks lifting cargo. You shouldn't need a qualified crane operator for this, but an extra set of hands might be helpful.) Once the cake is safely in place, pull the string out from under it.

Gently spoon the blue sugar into the gap between the tank and the cake. Sprinkle a layer on top. If you want little fish lips popping out the top of the tank, model these out of the rolled fondant. Feed it some cake crumbs while you're at it. To serve, scoop it out like a tiramisu.

E ven packing school lunch boxes in the morning can be a source of inspiration for me. These brightly coloured glossy pieces of dehydrated fruit wraps come in long strips, rectangles, and even dinosaur prints. They always remind me of pulled sugar, an art of the pastry chef which involves a process I was never game enough to attempt because of the third-degree burns to your hands it seemed to involve. So I've cheated and used squares of these multicoloured confections to resemble pulled-sugar ribbons and wrapped cakes.

Rectangular Cake

- 1 cake 30 cm long, 20 cm wide and 3 cm high ($12 \times 8 \times 1\frac{1}{4}$ in), cut in half and stacked on top of each other to make 1 cake 20 cm long, 15 cm wide and 6 cm high ($8 \times 6 \times 2\frac{1}{2}$ in)
- $\frac{1}{2}$ quantity topcoat frosting (page 92) or chocolate butter (page 93)
- at least 15 multicoloured rectangles of dehydrated fruit snacks, each 10 cm (4 in) long and 8 cm (3 in) wide

Round Cake

- 2 round cakes, each 10 cm (4 in) across and 3 cm ($1\frac{1}{4}$ in) high
- $\frac{1}{2}$ quantity topcoat frosting (page 92) or chocolate butter (page 93)
- approximately 15 or more multicoloured rectangles of dehydrated fruit snacks, each 10 cm (4 in) long and 8 cm (3 in) wide

Instructions

Stack the cakes on top of each other, filling between the layers with some of the frosting or chocolate butter. Spread the remaining frosting or chocolate butter on the cake.

Place the rectangles of fruit directly against the sides and around the top edges of the cake, applying them directly to the frosting or chocolate butter. Use a knife or spatula to tuck in the bottom edges neatly. When you go around a corner on the rectangular cake or around the round cake, gather in the top edge of the fruit rectangle to keep the bottom part looking smooth around the 'bend'.

To make the bow loops, fold a rectangle of fruit in half widthways. Using your fingers, pleat the raw edge together. Then give it a good squeeze to hold it together as a bow loop. Put the loops in the refrigerator as you make them to help them keep their shape as any humidity tends to flatten them out.

Arrange the bow loops on the cake as shown and then refrigerate the cake to prevent humidity flattening the bow loops. When ready to serve, use a thin sharp *heated* knife to slice the cake.

More Ideas

- The thin strips of dehydrated fruit snacks that come in a 1 metre (3 ft) roll are lots of fun to work with as well. Try your hand at woven patterns by weaving a 'mat' (remember second-grade art class?) from these different coloured strips and covering a cake with it.
- Also try patterns of plaid, polka dots, stripes, and more.

the sporting life

Fields of Play

Use *different-shaped* pieces of chocolate, bubblegum or other sweets or candy as basketballs, baseballs, tennis balls and golf balls.

A djust your playing field cake to match the flying balls. To get a very dark coloured frosting for your team colours, you will need to use paste or powder food colouring, available from cake decorating or chocolate supply shops. The problem with these dark colours is that they tend to bleed into other colours. I prefer to use ready-made sweets and candies, which are already intensely coloured, and simply apply them to the frosting in a pattern, for example, black and red licorice straps green, blue and yellow M&Ms, and so on.

For this cake you should use a medium-density cake such as a butter cake or denser so that the weight of the chocolate-covered almonds on the wires doesn't tear the cake.

Ingredients

- 1 cake (butter cake or denser), 33 cm long, 23 cm wide
and 3.5 cm high (13 × 9 × 1½ in)
- 1½ quantities topcoat frosting (page 92)
or ½ quantity crumbcoat frosting (page 92)
and 1 quantity topcoat frosting
- black licorice strips
- approximately 25 chocolate-covered almonds
- craft wire
- approximately 1½ cups green shredded dried coconut (page 96)

Instructions

Set aside 2 tbsp of the topcoat frosting for making football laces on the chocolate almonds.

Cut the cake in half so that you have two 23 cm long and 16 cm wide (9 × 6½ in) cakes. Stack the cakes on top of each other and fill between the layers with some of the topcoat frosting.

Spread the remaining topcoat frosting on the cake or, for a crumb-free frosting, first spread a thin layer of crumbcoat frosting on the cake and allow it to harden slightly for approximately an hour to 'set' the crumbs. Then spread the topcoat frosting on the cake (see page 92, Crumbs).

Attach the licorice strips to the cake or decorate the cake in your team's design with other decorations.

Sprinkle the green coconut on the cake. If you want, you can pipe lines on the playing field with frosting.

Heat the end of a craft wire and slide it into the end of a chocolate-covered almond. Allow the wired almond to rest for about 15 minutes until the chocolate sets around the wire.

Use a toothpick to trace laces or lines onto the football almonds with frosting. Decorate the cake with the footballs. Remove the wires before serving.

Divot

I don't know much about golf, but
I imagine this would be an annoying
shot for boys *big and small*. This little
masterpiece is best presented on a large
flat shovel in the middle of the cake table.
Sprinkle extra cake crumbs around it to
make it look like you just dug it fresh
from the golf green.

The white 'flag pole' is actually a candle to be lit when you are ready to sing. The white chocolate golf ball is made by Whitman's and is available at supermarkets, but you can buy them in the confectionery sections of many department stores.

Ingredients

- 1 chocolate cake, 30 cm long and 20 cm wide (12 × 8 in)
- 1½ quantities topcoat frosting (page 92)
- green food colouring (preferably paste or powder)
- white chocolate golf ball
- piping bag, leaf or star tip
- long thin white candle (or bamboo skewer)
- rice paper (available from baking section of supermarket or Asian grocery store) or plain paper
- food colouring to write message on flag

Instructions

Slice the edges off the cake to give it a rough appearance, as if it has been dug out of the ground. Crumble the offcuts with your hands or by pulsing in a food processor and scatter this 'soil' around the cake once it is decorated.

Set aside 2 tbsp of frosting for writing a message on the flag. Colour the remaining frosting green and spread a thin layer on the cake. Use a round cutter to cut a golf-ball sized hole in the cake.

Fill a piping bag fitted with a leaf or star-like tip with the green frosting and pipe individual leaves or stars across the top of the cake, excluding the golf-ball hole. Place the golf ball next to the hole.

Cut a flag from a piece of rice paper and attach it to the candle with a dab of the reserved white frosting. (You can use real paper and write a message with a pen if you don't want to fuss with this part.) Colour the reserved 2 tbsp of frosting and pipe a message on the rice-paper flag. Remove candle or skewer before serving.

no boys allowed

Squealers

Offer these *little jewels* to a table full of girls, young or old, and listen to them squeal with delight. There's nothing like a miniature cake decorated with an array of all the things girls are made of … pink bubble gum, ribbons, flowers, sugar beads and jewels.

For these miniature cakes, I like to start with a baked cake 2.5 cm (1 in) high. I am particularly fond of a fluffy sponge cake as a base for this design, however, you can use just about any cake base.

Ingredients

- 1 cake, 33 cm long, 23 cm wide and 2.5 cm high ($13 \times 9 \times 1$ in)
- 500 g (1 lb) sifted pure icing sugar (confectioner's sugar)
- 4–8 tbsp hot water or a mixture of hot water and fruit juice
- assortment of sugar beads, flowers, bubble-gum strips, sweets (candy), coloured sugar, etc.
- topcoat frosting (page 92) for piping decorations
- piping bag, tips
- food colouring
- biscuit (cookie) cutters of various sizes and shapes (round, square, heart)
- bamboo skewers

Instructions

If possible, refrigerate the cake layer for at least an hour before cutting the shapes to make them easier to handle.

Cut the desired shapes from the cake. If you want to stack them together, do so now, then skewer them snugly together on a bamboo skewer. You can also skewer the single-layer unstacked cakes to make them easier to dip. Alternatively, you can simply pour the icing over the single-layer cakes.

Pour the hot water into the pure icing sugar (confectioner's sugar). Keep this bowl of icing warm by placing it inside of another bowl of hot water.

Grasping both ends of the skewer, hold a little cake sideways and immerse it in the bowl of icing, turning it to coat all sides. If the skewer is too long to fit into the bowl, just trim it with a pair of kitchen scissors. Rest it right side up on a baking rack, keeping the skewer in place, for approximately 20 minutes. Dip it a second time and rest on the baking rack again.

★ If you want to attach decorations to the icing while the icing is still wet, do so now. Otherwise you can wait for about an hour until they are dry and easier to handle, then use a dab of frosting to attach the decorations.

Remove the skewer from the cake and decorate. There will be a little hole in the top of the cake from the skewer. That's a spot for a decoration!

More Ideas

• Use miniature objects such as Barbie doll furniture
(little tables and chairs) as individual cake stands.
• For my daughter's birthday, I used an assortment of mismatched silver,
brass, and glass candlestick holders as a holder to support these little cakes.
I also found some ornate, jewel-like napkin-ring holders and used
them as a stand . . . double squeals!

Tea Party

I created a teapot cake and made the teacups to go with it for my daughter *Georgina's* fifth birthday party.

T he teacups are china demitasse cups on which you pipe frosting decorations. The cups are then filled with crumbled sponge and flavouring, and sealed with chocolate butter to resemble coffee. Use tiramisu, trifles, no-bake cheesecakes, and mousses instead of the sponges if you like.

Ingredients

- 1 sponge cake, 33 cm long, 23 cm wide and 3.5 cm (13 × 9 × 1½ in)
- 1 quantity chocolate butter (page 93) at liquid pouring consistency
- 12 china demitasse cups
- topcoat frosting (page 92) for piping decorations on the cups
- food colouring
- piping bag, tips
- sugar beads or decorations
- coloured sugar (page 96)
- 1 cup water
- paint brush
- ½ cup sugar
- flavouring: for 'big' girls, dissolve 1 tbsp instant coffee with 1 tbsp boiling water; for little girls, try a teaspoon of strawberry, mint or orange extract

Instructions

Colour the frosting as desired. Fill a piping bag with the frosting and pipe decorations directly onto the teacups.

Paint the edge of the saucers with water, then dip them in coloured sugar. Allow to rest for half an hour.

Heat the water and ½ cup of sugar until the sugar dissolves. Allow to cool, then add the flavouring.

Break up the sponge into small bite-size pieces and place in a large bowl. Sprinkle the flavoured sugar syrup mixture over the sponge pieces and toss to coat evenly. Fill the cups approximately ¾ full with the sponge mixture.

Pour the liquid chocolate butter over the sponge to seal it. (Do not allow it to thicken to spreading consistency. If it does, just reheat it.) Store in the refrigerator. Remove from the refrigerator approximately one hour before serving and serve at room temperature.

Teapot

I don't expect you to whip up this cake as I have with all the other designs in this book. It is quite advanced, but it looked *so gorgeous* with the little teacups that I just had to include it.

Y ou'll need a dense cake base for this design to hold the handle and spout.

Ingredients

- 4 round chocolate fudge cakes (page 90), each 20 cm (8 in) across and 3 cm (1¼ in) high
- 2 quantities chocolate butter (page 93)
- 1½ quantities rolled fondant (three 500 g/1 lb boxes, if purchasing)
- yellow food colouring (preferably paste)
- sifted pure icing sugar (confectioner's sugar) for dusting work surface
- craft wire
- 1 quantity sugar dough (page 94) or quick sugar dough (page 95)
- yellow sugar beads
- 1 large sugar rose and leaves★
- ½ quantity topcoat frosting (page 92)
- piping bag, various tips
- green, yellow, pink, and purple food colouring
- small round cutters for spout petals

★ For a complete lesson on sugar flower making, see my book, *Cakes in Bloom* (Allen & Unwin, 1993, 1996, 1998)

Instructions

Stack the cakes on top of each other, filling between the layers with ¾ of the chocolate butter.

Carve the top of the cake with a thin, sharp knife to resemble the teapot shape shown. Spread the remaining chocolate butter over the cake.

Colour the rolled fondant pale yellow. Dust your work surface generously with the sifted pure icing sugar (confectioner's sugar). Knead the rolled fondant until it is nice and smooth. Form it into a ball and begin to flatten it with your hands into a circle. Use the rolling pin to finish the flattening. Ideally the rolled fondant should be approximately 1 cm (½ in) thick, but if this is your first time working with it you may want to make it thicker so it's easier to handle. Fold it over the rolling pin and lift it onto the cake. Smooth it over the cake, beginning at the top and working your way down the sides. Trim excess rolled fondant and smooth the bottom edges under with a knife or spatula (or if you have professional cake-decorating smoothing tools for this, by all means, bring 'em out).

To make the handle, bend a craft wire into the shape of a handle and cover it with a thick 'sausage' of green sugar dough, leaving 5 cm (2 in) of wire exposed at both ends. Position the handle on the cake and press the exposed wire ends into the cake. Remember to remove the handle and wire before serving!

To make the spout, bend a craft wire in half so that you have the two ends of the wire at one end, spread apart approximately 2 cm (¾ in). Shape this wire into a spout and cover it with a thin sausage of pale yellow sugar dough, leaving approximately 5 cm (2 in) of wire exposed at the bottom of the spout. Roll out some sugar dough to a thickness of 1.5 mm (⅟₁₆ in) or less and cut out round shapes for the petals on the spout. Work with one petal at a time, smoothing the edges of each petal between your thumb and middle and index fingers to give it movement. Starting at the top of the spot, wrap the first petal around the tip of the spout tightly (like a closed bud), using water to attach it. Continue down the spout until it is covered in petals. Carefully insert the spout into the teapot. Brush the area lightly with water where the spout joins the cake for added strength. Remember to remove the spout and wire before serving!

Colour the frosting and pipe decorations on the teapot using different tips.

Attach the yellow sugar beads around the teapot with a dot of frosting. Attach the green sugar leaves at the top of the handle. Place the sugar rose on top of the teapot.

basics

Ingredients and Materials

Cornflour
Use cornflour (cornstarch), the fine white thickening powder, not polenta, the coarse yellow cornmeal, to hold sugar flowers while they dry.

Edible Flowers
Edible flowers include: unsprayed pesticide-free apple blossom, lemon blossom, lilacs, nasturtiums, orange blossom, pansies, petunias, roses and violets.

Food Colouring
Liquid food colouring, available from the supermarket, is used to colour frosting, rolled fondant and sugar dough and to paint *dry* sugar dough decorations. Paste and powder food colouring, available from cake decorating, craft or pastry supply shops, does not dilute your mixture as much as liquid food colouring. It is great for getting intense dark or bright colours.

Glucose and Glycerine
Glucose and glycerine are available from cake decorating shops, chemists or drug stores. (Light corn syrup can be substituted for glucose.)

Cake Bases

For decorated cakes, I prefer a cake that can be made in advance and left at cool room temperature to avoid taking up space in the refrigerator. The chocolate fudge cake, frostings, chocolate butter and rolled fondant can all keep at cool room temperature for at least three days.

You can use almost any sponge, butter, or other recipe unless I specify that you need a specific type of cake. Some of the designs are 'piled high' and require a dense cake: 'dense' as in 'denser than your average butter cake'.

Many chocolate tortes, fruitcakes, puddings, and mud cakes will suffice for the designs that require a dense cake, but be careful—all the words I have just mentioned have been misused more than I can recall. If you aren't sure, use my chocolate fudge cake when you need a dense cake.

Chocolate Fudge Cake

This is a rich, dense cake that resembles baked fudge more than a cake. A small serve goes a long way! These cakes yield a thinner cake (approximately 3 cm/1¼ in high) than your usual butter cakes and sponges. Use it whenever a design calls for a dense cake. This recipe makes 1 round cake 25 cm (10 in) across and 3 cm (1¼ in) high.

Ingredients

- 60 g (2 oz) semi-sweet chocolate   • 350 g (12 oz) unsalted butter
- 60 g (2 oz) Dutch processed cocoa (not drinking cocoa, check the box)
- 60 ml (¼ cup) boiling water   • 400 g (14 oz) sugar
- 3 large (#61) eggs   • ½ tsp salt   • 200 g (7 oz) plain flour

Instructions

Preheat oven to 180°C (350°F). Butter and flour the cake tin. Cut out a piece of baking paper to fit the tin and place it in the tin. Place the butter and chocolate in a heatproof bowl over (not in) simmering water and heat until the chocolate melts and the butter is hot to touch. This can also be done in the microwave by heating at medium power for 40-second intervals, stirring in between each interval. Place the cocoa in a large mixing bowl. Pour the boiling water over the cocoa mixture, and stir. Pour the hot butter mixture over the cocoa, and stir. Stir in the sugar. Add the eggs one at a time, stirring after each addition. Add the salt and flour, and stir. Beat on high speed for 1 minute.

Fill your cake tin 2.5 cm (1 in) high with the batter and bake. I have given baking times below, but the best way to tell if the cake is done is when a big crack (or two) appears on the top of the cake and the cake barely wobbles when you shake the tin. (Don't bother inserting a toothpick, it will never come out clean!) Allow the cake to cool in the tin for 20 minutes, levelling the cake in the tin if it is uneven by pressing down with your fingers on the uneven edges. Loosen the sides of the tin with a spatula. Invert onto a cooling rack and allow to cool completely, preferably overnight, before decorating.

Butter Cake

This is a good, all-purpose butter cake. Once frosted, it will stay fresh for approximately two days at room temperature.

Ingredients

- 200 g (7 oz) unsalted butter   • 260 g (9 oz) sugar
- 2 large eggs   • 1½ tsp pure vanilla essence
- 260 g (9 oz) plain flour   • 4 tsp baking powder
- 1 tsp salt   • 190 ml (¾ cup) milk

Instructions

Preheat the over to 130°C (350°F). Butter and flour the cake tin. Cut out a piece of baking paper to fit the bottom of the cake tin and place it in the tin. Beat the butter and sugar together until light and fluffy. Add the eggs one at a time. Add the vanilla. Sift the flour, baking powder and salt into a small bowl. Add, alternately, the flour mixture and milk to the batter. Beat for 1 minute. Pour into the prepared tin and smooth the top with a spatula so that it is even. The batter should half fill a 5 cm (2 in) tin (so it should come up 2.5 cm (1 in) in your tin). Bake according to the chart on this page. To test for doneness, insert a toothpick; it should come out clean. Allow the baked cake to rest on a wire cake rack for 10 minutes. Loosen the sides of the tin by running a spatula around it. Invert onto the cooling rack and allow to cool completely.
Note: if you want to slice off the rounded top, it is best to refrigerate the cake for about an hour before doing so to make it easier to slice.

Baking Times and Tin Sizes

The tins I use for this cake are 5 cm (2 in) high. Filling the cake tin 2.5 cm (1 in) high will give you a baked cake of approximately 3 cm (1¼ in) high for the chocolate fudge and 3.5 cm (1½ in) for the butter cake (once you slice off the rounded top). Note that fan-forced ovens require 5–10 minutes less baking time.

Tin (Pan)		Baking Time (Chocolate Fudge)	Baking Time (Butter Cake)	Quantity of Recipe Required
Round	Round			
15 cm	6 in	30 min	20 min ⅓	
18 cm	7 in	35 min	25 min ½	
20 cm	8 in	40 min	25 min ⅔	
23 cm	9 in	45 min	30 min (just over ¾)	
25 cm	10 in	50 min	35 min 1	
Rectangular	Rectangular			
33 × 23 cm	13 × 9 in	55 min	35 min 1 (only bakes to 2.2 cm (⅞ in) high)	
30 × 20 cm	12 × 8 in	50 min	30 min 1 (only bakes to 2.5 cm (1 in) high)	
Cupcakes (12-hole muffin tin)		20 min	1	

To calculate the quantity of the recipe you will need for a square, multiply the quantity required for a round version by 1.33 (i.e., a 25 cm/10 in square requires 1 (the quantity of a 25 cm/10 in round) × 1.33 = 1.33 (1⅓) of the recipe).

Frostings, Fillings and Coverings

Crumbs

First, a word or two about *crumbs*. People generally love making birthday cakes for their children but the most common complaint is about crumbs in the frosting. Here is the answer. When you paint a wall you have to first fill in any holes with plaster and give it a base coat before you apply your smooth topcoat. Well, it's the same thing with frosting a cake. First you have to give your cake a crumbcoat with a thinner, less creamy frosting to 'set' the crumbs, then you give it a thicker, creamier topcoat. Please note that many of the designs in this book do not require this two-step process because the cake (crumbs included) is covered in decorations.

Crumbcoat Frosting

Ingredients

• 50 g (1½ oz) unsalted butter at room temperature   • 500 g (1 lb) pure icing sugar (confectioner's sugar)
• 60 ml (¼ cup) or more water

Instructions

Mix together the butter and sugar. Add the water gradually, mixing until all the ingredients are incorporated. Beat at high speed for 5 minutes.

Spread a thin layer of this frosting over the cake allowing it to harden and form a crust so that the crumbs 'set'. This may take an hour or two, depending on the humidity (you can cheat and speed up the process by putting the cake in the refrigerator, but the cake is likely to 'sweat' when you take it out of the refrigerator). Once set, apply topcoat frosting.

Topcoat Frosting

This is a thicker, creamier frosting which you use if you are doing a topcoat or just a single layer of frosting (with no crumbcoat).

Ingredients

• 150 g (5 oz) or more unsalted butter at room temperature
• 500 g (1 lb) pure icing sugar (confectioner's sugar)
• 1 tsp vanilla extract (optional)   • 60 ml (¼ cup) or more water

Instructions

Beat the butter in a bowl until nice and fluffy. Add the sugar, vanilla and water. Beat for 5 minutes until fluffy and light. I prefer a spreading consistency somewhere between soft and stiff peak. If too thin, add more sugar. If too thick, add more water.

Chocolate Butter

Chocolate and butter—a simple but perfect combination for spreading over a cake or between its layers.

Ingredients

• 300 g (10 oz) semi-sweet chocolate   • 250 g (8 oz) unsalted butter

Instructions

Place the butter and chocolate in a heatproof bowl over (not in) simmering water and heat until almost completely melted. This can also be done in the microwave by heating at medium power for 30 second intervals, stirring in between each interval. Remove from heat and stir until completely melted.

Allow to sit at room temperature until it reaches a smooth spreading consistency (an hour or so depending on your room temperature).

Rolled Fondant

Also called soft icing, pettinice, plastic icing, ready-to-roll icing, but please note that it is not the same as poured fondant. This is a heavy dough which can be rolled out and used to cover a cake for a smooth, almost perfect finish. It forms a light crust on the outside after a few days, but remains soft on the inside. In Australia and England, almost all supermarkets carry this in 500 gram (1 lb) boxes. This is more convenient than making your own. Rolled fondant is becoming more popular in the United States and is available ready made from cake-decorating and pastry-supply shops. If you can't buy it, here's the recipe.

Ingredients

• 60 ml (¼ cup) water at room temperature   • 1 tbsp powdered gelatine
• ½ cup glucose (page 89; or light corn syrup)   • 1½ tbsp glycerine (page 89)
• 1 tbsp solid white vegetable shortening (or liquid vegetable oil)
• 1 tspn of flavouring if desired (colourless if you want white fondant)
• 1 kg (2 lb) sifted pure icing sugar (confectioner's sugar)

Sprinkle the gelatine over the water and stir gently to break up any lumps. Allow to rest for 5 minutes or until the gelatine has absorbed most of the water. Heat gently (do not boil) on low in the microwave or in a heatproof glass over simmering water just until the gelatine has dissolved. Remove from heat and add the gelatine mixture to the glucose, glycerine, shortening (or oil) and flavouring. Stir together.

Place three-quarters of the sifted sugar in a large bowl and make a well in the middle. Pour the liquid mixture into the well. Mix with a heavy wooden spoon (or your hands), starting in the middle and gradually bringing in more sugar until you can't add any more. Wrap the mixture in a plastic bag or plastic wrap then place in a bowl. Place in the microwave and heat on low for approximately 15 seconds to make it easier to work. Knead in the rest of the sugar then place in the microwave again for 15 seconds on medium, then knead until smooth. (If you do not have a microwave, cut the rolled fondant into cubes and knead each one until it is smooth and softened, then combine all the pieces and knead them together.) You should be able to press a finger into the dough and get a perfect indentation without it cracking or sticking to your finger. If the dough sticks to your finger, continue to add more sugar until it no longer sticks. The rolled fondant can be stored, well wrapped in plastic, in an airtight container at room temperature for three days.

Sugar Dough

Sugar dough is also called modelling paste, gum paste, pastillage, and a few other names. I call it sugar dough. I use it to model and sculpt elaborate edible flowers, leaves and decorations for my cakes. It dries hard but is fragile, so handle with care.

Ingredients

• 1/2 cup (125 ml) water at room temperature   • 1 tbsp plus 2 teaspoons powdered gelatine
• 1 tsp cream of tartar   • 500 g (1 lb) pure icing sugar (confectioner's sugar)
• 100 g (3 oz) cornflour (cornstarch)

Instructions

Sprinkle cream of tartar and gelatine over the water and stir gently to break up any lumps. Allow to rest for 5 minutes until the gelatine has absorbed most of the water. Heat gently (do not boil) on low in the microwave or in a heatproof glass over simmering water just until the gelatine has dissolved. Remove from heat. Place sugar and cornflour (cornstarch) in a large mixer bowl. Add the gelatine mixture and mix on low until all the ingredients are incorporated. Beat on high speed for 5 minutes until light and fluffy. Place in an airtight container and store in the refrigerator for up to a month.

To make sugar dough decorations, remove a piece of sugar dough and keep adding pure icing sugar (confectioner's sugar) or cornflour (cornstarch) until the sugar dough is soft and pliable like Play Doh and no longer sticks to your fingers.

Quick Sugar Dough

If you're able to buy boxes of rolled fondant (soft icing, pettinice, etc.) already made, here's a very quick way of making sugar dough. It doesn't dry as hard as the sugar dough recipe, but it works for the designs in this book.

Ingredients

• 500 g (1 lb) purchased fondant or rolled fondant (or half the rolled fondant recipe)
• approximately 90 g (3 oz) cornflour (cornstarch)

Instructions

Knead the cornflour into the rolled fondant and use as sugar dough

Sugar Syrup

Ingredients

• 60 g (2 oz) sugar • 125 ml (½ cup) water

Instructions

Heat the water and sugar together until the sugar dissolves. Cool the syrup to room temperature.

Techniques

Making Your Cake Level

Your decorated cake will be as level as the layers that go into creating it. The chocolate fudge cake, and most dense cakes, can be levelled in the tin 5 minutes after they are baked by simply pressing down the uneven parts. For butter and sponge cakes, it is best to refrigerate them first then slice off the uneven top with a long serrated knife. I can't remember the last time I ever had to slice off any cake to make it level. I usually fill between layers and match up high sides with low sides, pressing down as I go. Somehow, it always ends up level.

Frosting a Cake

Dust any loose crumbs off your cake with a pastry brush. Spread the frosting on the cake, applying it to the sides first, and then the top. Cake turntables or a lazy Susan make the job much easier. You can get an inexpensive plastic one in the kitchen section of most department stores. Here's how you use one of these properly: apply the frosting to the cake sides or top, hold the spatula in *one place* with *one hand* and *move the turntable* with the other hand.

Piping

Piping bags and tubes with tips are available from the baking or kitchen section of supermarkets. For the designs in this book, I've used the tips that come with a supermarket set. The best way to learn how to use the bag and tips is by experimenting with them on cake tins, piping vertically and horizontally at different angles to see how to make different shapes and patterns. Don't fill the piping bag too full with frosting—half full is plenty. Piping is a process of pressing and releasing. After a few minutes of practice, you should be able to do most of the piping in this book.

Colouring

To use liquid food colouring, add a drop at a time to frosting, rolled fondant or sugar dough, mixing or kneading until it is the correct shade. To use paste or powder food colouring, dip a toothpick into the colouring and add a 'dot' at a time to your mixture, mixing or kneading it in until it is the correct shade. For painting *dry* sugar dough decorations, dilute either liquid or paste food colouring with vodka to get a lighter shade of food colouring. The vodka helps the colouring dry quicker but if you don't have any on hand, you can use water to dilute it but it will take longer to dry.

Remember that with any food colouring, your frosting or decoration may get darker or lighter after it dries. Wear disposable plastic gloves to keep from staining your hands if you are kneading food colouring into rolled fondant or sugar dough.

Colouring Sugar

You can buy coloured sugar crystals in the baking section at many supermarkets, but it's easy to make your own by placing sugar (plain, white granulated sugar) in a bowl and adding a few drops of food colouring. Mix it up, rubbing between your hands to distribute the colour evenly.

Colouring Coconut

Place shredded dried coconut in a bowl and add a few drops of food colouring. Wet your hands lightly, shaking them almost dry, then mix it up, rubbing between your hands to distribute the colour evenly.